ROALD DAHL
CHARLIE AND THE CHOCOLATE FACTORY
MAD LIBS

by Leigh Olsen

MAD LIBS
Penguin Young Readers Group
An Imprint of Penguin Random House LLC

Mad Libs format copyright © 2018 by Penguin Random House LLC. All rights reserved.

Concept created by Roger Price & Leonard Stern

Copyright © 2018 by The Roald Dahl Story Company Limited
Illustrations copyright © 1998 by Quentin Blake

Published in 2018 by Mad Libs,
an imprint of Penguin Random House LLC,
345 Hudson Street, New York, New York 10014.
Printed in the USA.

Penguin supports copyright. Copyright fuels creativity, encourages diverse voices,
promotes free speech, and creates a vibrant culture. Thank you for buying an authorized
edition of this book and for complying with copyright laws by not reproducing, scanning,
or distributing any part of it in any form without permission. You are supporting writers
and allowing Penguin to continue to publish books for every reader.

ISBN 9781524787158
3 5 7 9 10 8 6 4 2

MAD LIBS is a registered trademark of Penguin Random House LLC.

MAD LIBS
INSTRUCTIONS

MAD LIBS® is a game for people who don't like games! It can be played by one, two, three, four, or forty.

• RIDICULOUSLY SIMPLE DIRECTIONS

In this tablet you will find stories containing blank spaces where words are left out. One player, the READER, selects one of these stories. The READER does not tell anyone what the story is about. Instead, he/she asks the other players, the WRITERS, to give him/her words. These words are used to fill in the blank spaces in the story.

• TO PLAY

The READER asks each WRITER in turn to call out a word—an adjective or a noun or whatever the space calls for—and uses them to fill in the blank spaces in the story. The result is a MAD LIBS® game.

When the READER then reads the completed MAD LIBS® game to the other players, they will discover that they have written a story that is fantastic, screamingly funny, shocking, silly, crazy, or just plain dumb—depending upon which words each WRITER called out.

• EXAMPLE (*Before* and *After*)

"_____!" he said _____
    EXCLAMATION   ADVERB

as he jumped into his convertible _____ and
                                            NOUN

drove off with his _____ wife.
                      ADJECTIVE

"**OUCH**!" he said **STUPIDLY**
  EXCLAMATION   ADVERB

as he jumped into his convertible **CAT** and
                                          NOUN

drove off with his **BRAVE** wife.
                      ADJECTIVE

MAD LIBS
QUICK REVIEW

In case you have forgotten what adjectives, adverbs, nouns, and verbs are, here is a quick review:

An ADJECTIVE describes something or somebody. *Lumpy, soft, ugly, messy,* and *short* are adjectives.

An ADVERB tells how something is done. It modifies a verb and usually ends in "ly." *Modestly, stupidly, greedily,* and *carefully* are adverbs.

A NOUN is the name of a person, place, or thing. *Sidewalk, umbrella, bridle, bathtub,* and *nose* are nouns.

A VERB is an action word. *Run, pitch, jump,* and *swim* are verbs. Put the verbs in past tense if the directions say PAST TENSE. *Ran, pitched, jumped,* and *swam* are verbs in the past tense.

When we ask for A PLACE, we mean any sort of place: a country or city (*Spain, Cleveland*) or a room (*bathroom, kitchen*).

An EXCLAMATION or SILLY WORD is any sort of funny sound, gasp, grunt, or outcry, like *Wow!, Ouch!, Whomp!, Ick!,* and *Gadzooks!*

When we ask for specific words, like a NUMBER, a COLOR, an ANIMAL, or a PART OF THE BODY, we mean a word that is one of those things, like *seven, blue, horse,* or *head.*

When we ask for a PLURAL, it means more than one. For example, *cat* pluralized is *cats.*

MAD LIBS® is fun to play with friends, but you can also play it by yourself! To begin with, DO NOT look at the story on the page below. Fill in the blanks on this page with the words called for. Then, using the words you have selected, fill in the blank spaces in the story.

Now you've created your own hilarious MAD LIBS® game!

HERE COMES CHARLIE

NOUN _____

A PLACE _____

ADJECTIVE _____

ADJECTIVE _____

PLURAL NOUN _____

ADVERB _____

NOUN _____

NOUN _____

PLURAL NOUN _____

NOUN _____

NOUN _____

NOUN _____

PART OF THE BODY _____

ADJECTIVE _____

MAD LIBS®
HERE COMES CHARLIE

Charlie Bucket lived with his big family in a small wooden _____ (NOUN) on the edge of (the) _____ (A PLACE). He shared his home with his _____ (ADJECTIVE) parents, Mr. and Mrs. Bucket, and his four _____ (ADJECTIVE) grandparents, who all slept in one bed. His family was so poor, they didn't have two _____ (PLURAL NOUN) to rub together, but they loved one another _____ (ADVERB). Charlie's father, Mr. Bucket, worked day and _____ (NOUN) in a toothpaste factory. He made just enough money to feed his family bread with _____ (NOUN) for breakfast, boiled _____ (PLURAL NOUN) and cabbage for lunch, and cabbage _____ (NOUN) for supper. But for Charlie, who was a growing _____ (NOUN), it was never enough. The one thing he longed to eat more than anything else was a gigantic chocolate _____ (NOUN)! So you can imagine how Charlie's _____ (PART OF THE BODY) rumbled whenever he looked out the window and saw Willy Wonka's _____ (ADJECTIVE) chocolate factory. If only he could go inside!

From CHARLIE AND THE CHOCOLATE FACTORY MAD LIBS® • Copyright © 2018 by The Roald Dahl Story Company Limited. Published by Mad Libs, an imprint of Penguin Random House LLC.

MAD LIBS® is fun to play with friends, but you can also play it by yourself! To begin with, DO NOT look at the story on the page below. Fill in the blanks on this page with the words called for. Then, using the words you have selected, fill in the blank spaces in the story.

Now you've created your own hilarious MAD LIBS® game!

MR. WONKA'S FACTORY, BY GRANDPA JOE

NOUN _____

NUMBER _____

A PLACE _____

ADJECTIVE _____

ADJECTIVE _____

NOUN _____

NOUN _____

A PLACE _____

ADJECTIVE _____

PLURAL NOUN _____

SAME PLURAL NOUN _____

ADJECTIVE _____

ADJECTIVE _____

ADJECTIVE _____

MAD LIBS®
MR. WONKA'S FACTORY, BY GRANDPA JOE

Let me tell you the incredible true tale of Willy Wonka's _____
                                                            NOUN
factory! It is gigantic! In fact, it is _____ times bigger than any
                                         NUMBER
other chocolate factory in all of (the) _____. And Mr. Willy
                                          A PLACE
Wonka is the most _____ chocolate maker the world has ever
                    ADJECTIVE
seen! He can make anything out of chocolate—even a/an _____
                                                         ADJECTIVE
_____! Once, he made a huge chocolate _____ for
   NOUN   NOUN
an Indian prince to live in, but it melted, covering all of (the)
_____ in chocolate. But as magnificent as Mr. Wonka is, there
  A PLACE
is something very strange about his _____ factory. You see,
                                       ADJECTIVE
no _____ ever go in, and no _____ ever come
     PLURAL NOUN   SAME PLURAL NOUN
out. That's because, a long time ago, spies from other factories began
to sneak in and steal Mr. Wonka's _____ recipes! Now nobody
                                     ADJECTIVE
knows who—or what—is making Wonka's _____ chocolates.
                                          ADJECTIVE
It is one of the most _____ mysteries of the chocolate-making
                        ADJECTIVE
world!

MAD LIBS® is fun to play with friends, but you can also play it by yourself! To begin with, DO NOT look at the story on the page below. Fill in the blanks on this page with the words called for. Then, using the words you have selected, fill in the blank spaces in the story.

Now you've created your own hilarious MAD LIBS® game!

WONKA FACTORY TO OPEN

FIRST NAME (MALE) _____

NOUN _____

PART OF THE BODY (PLURAL) _____

ADJECTIVE _____

PLURAL NOUN _____

PLURAL NOUN _____

A PLACE _____

NOUN _____

ADJECTIVE _____

FIRST NAME (MALE) _____

A PLACE _____

PLURAL NOUN _____

PLURAL NOUN _____

VERB _____

MAD LIBS

WONKA FACTORY TO OPEN

Mr. _____ Wonka, the _____-making genius
    FIRST NAME (MALE)   NOUN

whom nobody has seen with their own _____ for
                                         PART OF THE BODY (PLURAL)

the last ten years, has made a/an _____ announcement: He is
                                ADJECTIVE

going to open his factory to five lucky _____! Five Golden
                                       PLURAL NOUN

_____ will be hidden inside five ordinary chocolate bars.
PLURAL NOUN

The bars may be for sale in any shop on any street in any town in any

_____ in the world! And whoever finds the tickets wins the
A PLACE

_____ of a lifetime. The _____ winners will be given
NOUN   ADJECTIVE

a tour of the factory by Mr. _____ Wonka himself! They
                                FIRST NAME (MALE)

will be among the only people in (the) _____ to ever lay eyes
                                          A PLACE

on the secrets and magical _____ inside the factory walls.
                                PLURAL NOUN

Each winner will receive a lifetime supply of _____! So
                                                PLURAL NOUN

run, don't _____, to your nearest Wonka retailer before it's
             VERB

too late!

MAD LIBS® is fun to play with friends, but you can also play it by yourself! To begin with, DO NOT look at the story on the page below. Fill in the blanks on this page with the words called for. Then, using the words you have selected, fill in the blank spaces in the story.

Now you've created your own hilarious MAD LIBS® game!

I'VE GOT A GOLDEN TICKET

ADJECTIVE _____

PART OF THE BODY _____

PLURAL NOUN _____

ADVERB _____

SILLY WORD _____

ADJECTIVE _____

VERB _____

ADJECTIVE _____

VERB _____

PLURAL NOUN _____

PLURAL NOUN _____

NUMBER _____

NOUN _____

NOUN _____

ADJECTIVE _____

MAD LIBS®

I'VE GOT A GOLDEN TICKET

Greetings to you, the _____ finder of this Golden Ticket,
                        ADJECTIVE

from Mr. Willy Wonka! I shake you warmly by the _____!
                                                 PART OF THE BODY

Many wonderful _____ await you! I would like to
                 PLURAL NOUN

_____ invite you to come to my factory, where I, Willy
   ADVERB

_____, will show you everything there is to see. Prepare
  SILLY WORD

yourself for marvelous and _____ surprises that will entrance,
                              ADJECTIVE

delight, intrigue, astonish, and _____ you beyond measure! In
                                     VERB

your most _____ dreams, you could never imagine such
            ADJECTIVE

things could happen to you. Just wait and _____! Then, at
                                               VERB

the end of the day, you will be sent home with a delicious supply of

_____ for you and your closest _____ to eat for
 PLURAL NOUN   PLURAL NOUN

the rest of your lives! On the first day of February, at _____
                                                           NUMBER

o'clock sharp, please bring your Golden _____ to the factory
                                           NOUN

gates. You are allowed to bring one _____ with you. Don't be
                                        NOUN

_____!
  ADJECTIVE

MAD LIBS® is fun to play with friends, but you can also play it by yourself! To begin with, DO NOT look at the story on the page below. Fill in the blanks on this page with the words called for. Then, using the words you have selected, fill in the blank spaces in the story.

Now you've created your own hilarious MAD LIBS® game!

WONKA'S WONDERFUL CHOCOLATES

PART OF THE BODY _____

NOUN _____

PART OF THE BODY _____

SILLY WORD _____

VERB _____

VERB ENDING IN "ING" _____

ADJECTIVE _____

NOUN _____

NOUN _____

SILLY WORD _____

NOUN _____

ADJECTIVE _____

PART OF THE BODY _____

ANIMAL _____

MAD LIBS®
WONKA'S WONDERFUL CHOCOLATES

The following are a few popular Wonka chocolates to tickle your imagination and delight your _____:
PART OF THE BODY

- Wonka's Whipple-Scrumptious Fudgemallow Delight is made of 100 percent pure _____ chocolate that melts in your _____!
  NOUN
  PART OF THE BODY

- Wonka's _____ Caramels change color every ten seconds while you _____.
  SILLY WORD
  VERB

- Wonka's _____ Gum never loses its _____ flavor.
  VERB ENDING IN "ING"
  ADJECTIVE

- Wonka's _____ Balloons can blow up to enormous sizes before you pop them with a/an _____ and gobble them up.
  NOUN
  NOUN

- Wonka's _____ Eggs look like a/an _____'s eggs with _____ spots on them, and when you put one in your _____, it gets smaller and smaller, until all that's left is a tiny pink sugary baby _____ sitting on the tip of your tongue!
  SILLY WORD
  NOUN
  ADJECTIVE
  PART OF THE BODY
  ANIMAL

MAD LIBS® is fun to play with friends, but you can also play it by yourself! To begin with, DO NOT look at the story on the page below. Fill in the blanks on this page with the words called for. Then, using the words you have selected, fill in the blank spaces in the story.

Now you've created your own hilarious MAD LIBS® game!

THE LUCKY FIVE

PLURAL NOUN _____

ADJECTIVE _____

A PLACE _____

PLURAL NOUN _____

NOUN _____

A PLACE _____

PART OF THE BODY _____

NOUN _____

A PLACE _____

ADVERB _____

NUMBER _____

A PLACE _____

NUMBER _____

PART OF THE BODY _____

PLURAL NOUN _____

ADJECTIVE _____

PART OF THE BODY _____

MAD LIBS
THE LUCKY FIVE

Meet the five winners of Willy Wonka's Golden _____!

PLURAL NOUN

- Augustus Gloop is an enormously _____ boy from (the)

ADJECTIVE
_____. Eating _____ is his favorite hobby.

A PLACE PLURAL NOUN

- Veruca Salt is a spoiled-rotten _____ from (the)

NOUN
_____, who has her parents wrapped around her little

A PLACE
_____.

PART OF THE BODY

- Violet Beauregarde is a dim-witted _____ from (the)

NOUN
_____ who talks very _____ and chews gum

A PLACE ADVERB
twenty-four hours a day, _____ days a week.

NUMBER

- Mike Teavee, who lives in (the) _____, carries _____

A PLACE NUMBER
toy pistols on a belt on his _____. He is obsessed with

PART OF THE BODY
watching _____ on television.

PLURAL NOUN

- Charlie Bucket is honest and kind, brave and _____, and

ADJECTIVE
has a/an _____ of gold!

PART OF THE BODY

From CHARLIE AND THE CHOCOLATE FACTORY MAD LIBS® • Copyright © 2018 by
The Roald Dahl Story Company Limited. Published by Mad Libs, an imprint of Penguin Random House LLC.

MAD LIBS® is fun to play with friends, but you can also play it by yourself! To begin with, DO NOT look at the story on the page below. Fill in the blanks on this page with the words called for. Then, using the words you have selected, fill in the blank spaces in the story.

Now you've created your own hilarious MAD LIBS® game!

VIOLET'S GUM-CHEWING SECRETS

PART OF THE BODY _____

NOUN _____

NUMBER _____

NOUN _____

ADJECTIVE _____

PART OF THE BODY _____

NOUN _____

NOUN _____

NOUN _____

PART OF THE BODY _____

NOUN _____

ADJECTIVE _____

PART OF THE BODY _____

NOUN _____

MAD LIBS
VIOLET'S GUM-CHEWING SECRETS

I, Violet Beauregarde, just *adore* chewing gum. I simply wouldn't feel comfortable if I didn't have a piece of gum in my _____ every
                                                                              PART OF THE BODY
moment of the day. In fact, it may interest you to know that this piece of _____ I'm chewing right now is one I've been working on
              NOUN
for _____ months solid. It's my own personal record. My secret
     NUMBER
is that at night, I place the wad of chewed _____ on my
                                                  NOUN
bedpost. In the morning, it tastes a little _____, but it softens
                                              ADJECTIVE
up again after I put it back in my _____. Before I began trying
                                    PART OF THE BODY
to beat the world record for _____ chewing, I used to chew a
                                 NOUN
single piece of _____ each day. I loved to put the chewed-up
                    NOUN
_____ on an elevator button so people would accidentally put
   NOUN
their _____ right on my gooey wad of _____! Ha ha!
      PART OF THE BODY   NOUN
Anyway, those are my most _____ gum-chewing secrets. If
                              ADJECTIVE
you put your _____ to it, you can beat your own personal
              PART OF THE BODY
record for _____ chewing, too!
              NOUN

MAD LIBS® is fun to play with friends, but you can also play it by yourself! To begin with, DO NOT look at the story on the page below. Fill in the blanks on this page with the words called for. Then, using the words you have selected, fill in the blank spaces in the story.

Now you've created your own hilarious MAD LIBS® game!

MEET MR. WILLY WONKA

ADJECTIVE _____

COLOR _____

NOUN _____

PART OF THE BODY _____

PART OF THE BODY (PLURAL) _____

PART OF THE BODY (PLURAL) _____

ADJECTIVE _____

NOUN _____

PLURAL NOUN _____

ADJECTIVE _____

PART OF THE BODY _____

ADJECTIVE _____

PLURAL NOUN _____

MAD LIBS

MEET MR. WILLY WONKA

When Charlie and the other ticket winners approached the chocolate factory, they were greeted by a/an _____ little man leaning on
_{ADJECTIVE}

a fancy _____ cane. He wore a/an _____ on his head,
_{COLOR} _{NOUN}

a purple jacket on his _____, and green trousers on his
_{PART OF THE BODY}

_____. It was Mr. Willy Wonka! Wonka did a funny
_{PART OF THE BODY (PLURAL)}

little skipping dance and spread his _____ wide.
_{PART OF THE BODY (PLURAL)}

He said, "Welcome, my _____ friends! Welcome to my
_{ADJECTIVE}

_____. I'm delighted to meet you and your _____.
_{NOUN} _{PLURAL NOUN}

I'm overjoyed! Enraptured! I'm positively _____! All right,
_{ADJECTIVE}

now please follow my _____. It's time for our _____
_{PART OF THE BODY} _{ADJECTIVE}

tour. And *do* stick together. We don't want to lose any _____
_{PLURAL NOUN}

along the way!"

MAD LIBS® is fun to play with friends, but you can also play it by yourself! To begin with, DO NOT look at the story on the page below. Fill in the blanks on this page with the words called for. Then, using the words you have selected, fill in the blank spaces in the story.

Now you've created your own hilarious MAD LIBS® game!

YOUR VISIT TO WONKA'S FACTORY

PART OF THE BODY _____

VERB _____

A PLACE _____

ADJECTIVE _____

ADJECTIVE _____

VERB ENDING IN "ING" _____

PART OF THE BODY _____

ADJECTIVE _____

NOUN _____

ADJECTIVE _____

VERB ENDING IN "S" _____

PART OF THE BODY (PLURAL) _____

ADJECTIVE _____

VERB ENDING IN "ING" _____

NOUN _____

NOUN _____

NOUN _____

MAD LIBS®
YOUR VISIT TO WONKA'S FACTORY

Willy Wonka's factory is filled with wonders the _____ has
                                                   PART OF THE BODY
never seen! On your visit, you will _____ along a mazelike
                                          VERB
corridor that leads down into the depths of (the) _____. Once
                                                      A PLACE
there, you'll reach the _____ Chocolate Room. It contains a
                              ADJECTIVE
lush valley with a great river of _____ chocolate! What's more,
                                       ADJECTIVE
there's a tremendous waterfall _____ into the river
                                    VERB ENDING IN "ING"
below. Don't forget to keep a/an _____ out for the
                                       PART OF THE BODY
_____ Oompa-Loompas! Next, take a ride on a pink
  ADJECTIVE
_____ boat down the _____ chocolate river. Be
   NOUN   ADJECTIVE
warned: The boat _____ very quickly! Feast your
                    VERB ENDING IN "S"
_____ on the Inventing Room, the most important
PART OF THE BODY (PLURAL)
room in the entire _____ factory! Filled with pots and kettles
                       ADJECTIVE
boiling and _____, this is where Mr. Wonka's most
                VERB ENDING IN "ING"
secret and exciting inventions are made. There you'll even find the

Great Gum Machine, which can make chewing gum that tastes like an

entire meal of _____ soup, roast _____, and
                    NOUN   NOUN
_____-berry pie!
   NOUN

MAD LIBS® is fun to play with friends, but you can also play it by yourself! To begin with, DO NOT look at the story on the page below. Fill in the blanks on this page with the words called for. Then, using the words you have selected, fill in the blank spaces in the story.

Now you've created your own hilarious MAD LIBS® game!

YOUR VISIT TO WONKA'S FACTORY, CONTINUED

PLURAL NOUN _____

PART OF THE BODY (PLURAL) _____

A PLACE _____

EXCLAMATION _____

ANIMAL (PLURAL) _____

ADJECTIVE _____

ADJECTIVE _____

NOUN _____

PART OF THE BODY _____

ADJECTIVE _____

ADJECTIVE _____

PLURAL NOUN _____

MAD LIBS®
YOUR VISIT TO WONKA'S FACTORY, CONTINUED

After the Inventing Room, don't forget to take a peek inside the room containing square _____ that look round! These candies
        PLURAL NOUN
are square, but they have eyes on their _____, so
                                         PART OF THE BODY (PLURAL)
they can look all round (the) _____! _____! Be
                                A PLACE   EXCLAMATION
sure to visit the Nut Room, where one hundred _____
                                                  ANIMAL (PLURAL)
work around the clock shelling nuts. Then, take the _____
                                                         ADJECTIVE
Glass Elevator up and down and all around to the Television-Chocolate Room. Mr. Wonka has invented a system where he can send a/an _____ chocolate bar from the factory directly into a television
  ADJECTIVE
right in your very own _____! It boggles the _____!
                          NOUN   PART OF THE BODY
Enjoy your _____ adventure at Wonka's _____
               ADJECTIVE   ADJECTIVE
factory! Just be sure to follow the rules and avoid getting into trouble.

The most magical _____ await you!
                     PLURAL NOUN

MAD LIBS® is fun to play with friends, but you can also play it by yourself! To begin with, DO NOT look at the story on the page below. Fill in the blanks on this page with the words called for. Then, using the words you have selected, fill in the blank spaces in the story.

Now you've created your own hilarious MAD LIBS® game!

POOR AUGUSTUS GLOOP!

ADJECTIVE _____

A PLACE _____

PLURAL NOUN _____

NOUN _____

PLURAL NOUN _____

NOUN _____

ADJECTIVE _____

NOUN _____

PART OF THE BODY _____

ADVERB _____

ADJECTIVE _____

ADVERB _____

PART OF THE BODY _____

MAD LIBS®
POOR AUGUSTUS GLOOP!

Poor, _____ Augustus Gloop! It all began innocently enough.
     ADJECTIVE

His hometown of (the) _____ went wild when he won the
                      A PLACE

first Golden Ticket. They even held a parade of _____ in
                                                PLURAL NOUN

Augustus's honor! His mother was over the _____ with
                                           NOUN

excitement. "Augustus eats so many candy _____, I just
                                          PLURAL NOUN

knew he would find a Golden _____!" she exclaimed. But
                               NOUN

when Augustus arrived at Willy Wonka's factory, things turned

_____. He simply could not resist the river filled with
ADJECTIVE

delicious liquid _____. He knelt down to take a drink and fell
                  NOUN

_____-first into the river of chocolate! Then, Augustus was
PART OF THE BODY

sucked _____ into a glass pipe! Before anyone could save him,
        ADVERB

he was whisked away to a room where fudge was made. "My

_____ boy will be turned into fudge!" Mrs. Gloop shrieked
ADJECTIVE

_____. But Mr. Wonka just laughed. "He'll be perfectly safe!"
ADVERB

he assured Mrs. Gloop. "Don't worry your pretty little _____!"
                                                       PART OF THE BODY

From CHARLIE AND THE CHOCOLATE FACTORY MAD LIBS® • Copyright © 2018 by
The Roald Dahl Story Company Limited. Published by Mad Libs, an imprint of Penguin Random House LLC.

MAD LIBS® is fun to play with friends, but you can also play it by yourself! To begin with, DO NOT look at the story on the page below. Fill in the blanks on this page with the words called for. Then, using the words you have selected, fill in the blank spaces in the story.

Now you've created your own hilarious MAD LIBS® game!

THE OOMPA-LOOMPAS FROM LOOMPALAND

A PLACE _____

PART OF THE BODY (PLURAL) _____

PLURAL NOUN _____

NOUN _____

SAME NOUN _____

ADJECTIVE _____

NOUN _____

PART OF THE BODY (PLURAL) _____

VERB _____

ADVERB _____

PART OF THE BODY (PLURAL) _____

VERB ENDING IN "ING" _____

ADJECTIVE _____

PLURAL NOUN _____

NOUN _____

MAD LIBS®
THE OOMPA-LOOMPAS FROM LOOMPALAND

When I, Mr. Willy Wonka, took a visit to Loompaland, deep in the jungles of (the) _____ (A PLACE), I could hardly believe my _____ (PART OF THE BODY (PLURAL)). The most dangerous _____ (PLURAL NOUN) in the world lived there, including those terrible, wicked _____ (NOUN)-doodles. A/An _____ (SAME NOUN)-doodle would eat ten Oompa-Loompas for breakfast! The poor Oompa-Loompas were living in tree houses just to escape them! And they *longed* to eat cacao beans, which are used to make my _____ (ADJECTIVE) chocolate. They dreamed about them night and _____ (NOUN)! And so I decided to take fate into my own _____ (PART OF THE BODY (PLURAL)). I asked the Oompa-Loompas to come _____ (VERB) with me in my factory in exchange for all the cacao beans they could ever eat! The Oompa-Loompas _____ (ADVERB) agreed. Now, they all work here, wearing nothing but deerskins and leaves on their _____ (PART OF THE BODY (PLURAL)). They love music and _____ (VERB ENDING IN "ING"), and they sing _____ (ADJECTIVE) songs while they work. They're happy as _____ (PLURAL NOUN), and they'll never fear being eaten by a/an _____ (NOUN)-doodle again!

From CHARLIE AND THE CHOCOLATE FACTORY MAD LIBS® • Copyright © 2018 by The Roald Dahl Story Company Limited. Published by Mad Libs, an imprint of Penguin Random House LLC.

MAD LIBS® is fun to play with friends, but you can also play it by yourself! To begin with, DO NOT look at the story on the page below. Fill in the blanks on this page with the words called for. Then, using the words you have selected, fill in the blank spaces in the story.

Now you've created your own hilarious MAD LIBS® game!

POOR VIOLET BEAUREGARDE!

ADJECTIVE _____

NOUN _____

NOUN _____

PLURAL NOUN _____

ADJECTIVE _____

ADJECTIVE _____

ADJECTIVE _____

ADVERB _____

PART OF THE BODY _____

PART OF THE BODY _____

PART OF THE BODY (PLURAL) _____

ADVERB _____

NOUN _____

TYPE OF LIQUID _____

MAD LIBS
POOR VIOLET BEAUREGARDE!

Poor, _____ Violet Beauregarde! Violet is a fast-talking, gum-
         ADJECTIVE

chewing _____. When she heard about the Golden Ticket,
           NOUN

however, she switched from chewing _____ to eating candy
                                        NOUN

_____ instead. And, lo and behold, she found a/an
PLURAL NOUN

_____ Ticket! You can imagine Violet's delight upon
ADJECTIVE

discovering Willy Wonka's _____ Gum Machine. It fits an
                            ADJECTIVE

entire three-course meal into a single stick of _____ chewing
                                                  ADJECTIVE

gum! "I want the gum!" Violet said _____. Even though Mr.
                                      ADVERB

Wonka warned her that the recipe wasn't quite right, Violet put the

stick in her _____ and began to chew. But soon, Violet's
            PART OF THE BODY

_____ turned blue, and her _____ began
PART OF THE BODY   PART OF THE BODY (PLURAL)

to swell. "Violet, you're turning violet, Violet!" her mother yelled

_____. Violet was turning into a gigantic _____-berry!
  ADVERB   NOUN

Poor Violet! It's off to the Juicing Room to squeeze the _____
                                                         TYPE OF LIQUID

out of her and get her back to normal!

MAD LIBS® is fun to play with friends, but you can also play it by yourself! To begin with, DO NOT look at the story on the page below. Fill in the blanks on this page with the words called for. Then, using the words you have selected, fill in the blank spaces in the story.

Now you've created your own hilarious MAD LIBS® game!

WONKA'S WILD INVENTIONS

ADJECTIVE _____

PLURAL NOUN _____

ADJECTIVE _____

PART OF THE BODY _____

ADJECTIVE _____

TYPE OF LIQUID _____

ADJECTIVE _____

PART OF THE BODY _____

NOUN _____

PART OF THE BODY _____

PLURAL NOUN _____

PART OF THE BODY _____

MAD LIBS®
WONKA'S WILD INVENTIONS

Here are just a few of Willy Wonka's _____ inventions in
                                         ADJECTIVE
progress:

- Everlasting Gobstoppers are perfect for little _____
                                                    PLURAL NOUN
  without much pocket money. They are _____ candies
                                              ADJECTIVE
  that you can suck and suck and they'll never disappear!

- Eatable Marshmallow Pillows will make a comfortable place to rest
  your _____ at night, and they are also perfect for a/an
         PART OF THE BODY
  _____ midnight snack!
       ADJECTIVE

- Hair Toffee is a thick, purplish _____ that, when you
                                        TYPE OF LIQUID
  eat it, causes a brand-new luscious, thick, silky, _____
                                                           ADJECTIVE
  crop of hair to grow all over your _____!
                                         PART OF THE BODY

- Lickable Wallpaper for Nurseries has pictures of bananas, apples,
  oranges, and _____-berries all over it, and when you lick
                    NOUN
  them with your _____, they taste like _____!
                    PART OF THE BODY   PLURAL NOUN

- Hot Ice Creams for Cold Days warm up your _____ when
                                                  PART OF THE BODY
  it's freezing outside!

From CHARLIE AND THE CHOCOLATE FACTORY MAD LIBS® • Copyright © 2018 by
The Roald Dahl Story Company Limited. Published by Mad Libs, an imprint of Penguin Random House LLC.

MAD LIBS® is fun to play with friends, but you can also play it by yourself! To begin with, DO NOT look at the story on the page below. Fill in the blanks on this page with the words called for. Then, using the words you have selected, fill in the blank spaces in the story.

Now you've created your own hilarious MAD LIBS® game!

VERUCA SALT'S WISH LIST

NUMBER _____

ADJECTIVE _____

ADJECTIVE _____

A PLACE _____

PLURAL NOUN _____

PART OF THE BODY (PLURAL) _____

ANIMAL _____

A PLACE _____

PLURAL NOUN _____

VEHICLE _____

ADJECTIVE _____

A PLACE _____

NOUN _____

A PLACE _____

ADJECTIVE _____

COLOR _____

PART OF THE BODY _____

ADJECTIVE _____

MAD LIBS

VERUCA SALT'S WISH LIST

Dear Mummy and Daddy,

As you know, I am about to turn _____ years old. Here is what I
                                      NUMBER
would like for my _____ birthday:
                       ADJECTIVE
A/An _____ party at (the) _____ with a clown who
         ADJECTIVE   A PLACE
can juggle at least four _____, someone to paint people's
                               PLURAL NOUN
_____, and _____ rides. An all-expenses-
 PART OF THE BODY (PLURAL)   ANIMAL
paid trip to (the) luxurious _____ for me and my closest
                                  A PLACE
_____. A flying _____ with a/an _____
 PLURAL NOUN   VEHICLE   ADJECTIVE
chauffeur that will take me all over (the) _____ at a moment's
                                                A PLACE
_____. A vacation home on the soft sandy beaches of (the)
   NOUN
_____. A/An _____ unicorn with sparkly,
   A PLACE   ADJECTIVE
_____ wings. That is all! Thank you from the bottom of
   COLOR
my _____.
    PART OF THE BODY

Love,

Your _____ daughter, Veruca
       ADJECTIVE

From CHARLIE AND THE CHOCOLATE FACTORY MAD LIBS® • Copyright © 2018 by
The Roald Dahl Story Company Limited. Published by Mad Libs, an imprint of Penguin Random House LLC.

MAD LIBS® is fun to play with friends, but you can also play it by yourself! To begin with, DO NOT look at the story on the page below. Fill in the blanks on this page with the words called for. Then, using the words you have selected, fill in the blank spaces in the story.

Now you've created your own hilarious MAD LIBS® game!

POOR VERUCA SALT!

NOUN _____

PART OF THE BODY (PLURAL) _____

NOUN _____

ADJECTIVE _____

NOUN _____

ADJECTIVE _____

ADJECTIVE _____

PLURAL NOUN _____

NOUN _____

PART OF THE BODY _____

NOUN _____

PLURAL NOUN _____

NOUN _____

MAD LIBS
POOR VERUCA SALT!

Veruca Salt is a very wealthy little _____. She desperately
                                         NOUN
wanted to get her _____ on a Golden Ticket. So her
                   PART OF THE BODY (PLURAL)
father, who works in the _____ business, ordered his
                              NOUN
_____ employees to yank the wrappers off Wonka candy bars
 ADJECTIVE
until they found a Golden _____. But that wasn't enough for
                                NOUN
_____ Veruca Salt! When they visited the Nut Room at Mr.
 ADJECTIVE
Wonka's factory, Veruca discovered it was filled with _____
                                                        ADJECTIVE
little squirrels. They were shelling _____ for Wonka's candy
                                      PLURAL NOUN
bars! Being the spoiled little _____ she is, Veruca decided she
                                   NOUN
had to have a squirrel for herself! But when she entered the Nut Room,
one squirrel began tapping on her _____. Then they dumped
                                   PART OF THE BODY
her into a/an _____! "She's going where all the bad
                  NOUN
_____ go," said Mr. Wonka. "Down the garbage
 PLURAL NOUN
_____! But don't worry. She'll turn up sooner or later!"
  NOUN

From CHARLIE AND THE CHOCOLATE FACTORY MAD LIBS® • Copyright © 2018 by
The Roald Dahl Story Company Limited. Published by Mad Libs, an imprint of Penguin Random House LLC.

MAD LIBS® is fun to play with friends, but you can also play it by yourself! To begin with, DO NOT look at the story on the page below. Fill in the blanks on this page with the words called for. Then, using the words you have selected, fill in the blank spaces in the story.

Now you've created your own hilarious MAD LIBS® game!

WONKA'S TOP SECRET CHOCOLATE RECIPE

A PLACE _____

PART OF THE BODY (PLURAL) _____

NOUN _____

ADJECTIVE _____

PART OF THE BODY (PLURAL) _____

NOUN _____

NOUN _____

NOUN _____

A PLACE _____

NUMBER _____

NOUN _____

NOUN _____

ADJECTIVE _____

NOUN _____

ADVERB _____

ADJECTIVE _____

ADJECTIVE _____

NOUN _____

MAD LIBS®
WONKA'S TOP SECRET CHOCOLATE RECIPE

Every chocolate maker this side of (the) _____ wants to get their
                                          A PLACE

grubby little _____ on Willy Wonka's scrumdiddly-
              PART OF THE BODY (PLURAL)

umptious chocolate recipe. Mr. Wonka has to guard this precious

recipe with his _____! Lucky for you, he has decided to share
                    NOUN

his _____ recipe—for your _____ only:
    ADJECTIVE   PART OF THE BODY (PLURAL)

Gently melt a half cup of the finest quality _____ oil in a
                                                 NOUN

saucepan over low heat. Stir in a half cup of _____ powder,
                                                  NOUN

derived from organic _____ beans sourced from (the)
                         NOUN

_____. Add _____ tablespoons of honey, taken directly
  A PLACE   NUMBER

from a/an _____-hive. Then pour in a half teaspoon of
             NOUN

_____ extract and stir until the mixture has a/an _____
   NOUN   ADJECTIVE

consistency. Finally, for Mr. Willy Wonka's most secret ingredient, add

a dash of _____ powder and stir _____. Mold the
             NOUN   ADVERB

mixture into _____ shapes and allow to cool. Take a/an
              ADJECTIVE

_____ bite and enjoy the world's finest chocolate _____!
 ADJECTIVE   NOUN

From CHARLIE AND THE CHOCOLATE FACTORY MAD LIBS® • Copyright © 2018 by
The Roald Dahl Story Company Limited. Published by Mad Libs, an imprint of Penguin Random House LLC.

MAD LIBS® is fun to play with friends, but you can also play it by yourself! To begin with, DO NOT look at the story on the page below. Fill in the blanks on this page with the words called for. Then, using the words you have selected, fill in the blank spaces in the story.

Now you've created your own hilarious MAD LIBS® game!

THE OOMPA-LOOMPAS' SONG

YOUR NAME _____

NOUN _____

VERB ENDING IN "ING" _____

PLURAL NOUN _____

YOUR NAME _____

A PLACE _____

PLURAL NOUN _____

YOUR NAME _____

ADJECTIVE _____

NOUN _____

YOUR NAME _____

YOUR NAME _____

MAD LIBS
THE OOMPA-LOOMPAS' SONG

_____, the little brute,
YOUR NAME

Has just gone down the _____ chute.
NOUN

Please believe us when we say

That _____ _____ will never pay!
VERB ENDING IN "ING"   PLURAL NOUN

But _____ made a grave mistake
YOUR NAME

And has been sent off to (the) _____.
A PLACE

But don't, dear _____, be alarmed;
PLURAL NOUN

_____ will not be harmed!
YOUR NAME

What we do in cases such

As this, we use a/an _____ touch,
ADJECTIVE

And do something that, come what may,

Will take the child's _____ away!
NOUN

_____ is fine, now, don't you fret,
YOUR NAME

_____ will be even better, yet!
YOUR NAME

From CHARLIE AND THE CHOCOLATE FACTORY MAD LIBS® • Copyright © 2018 by
The Roald Dahl Story Company Limited. Published by Mad Libs, an imprint of Penguin Random House LLC.

MAD LIBS® is fun to play with friends, but you can also play it by yourself! To begin with, DO NOT look at the story on the page below. Fill in the blanks on this page with the words called for. Then, using the words you have selected, fill in the blank spaces in the story.

Now you've created your own hilarious MAD LIBS® game!

MIKE TEAVEE'S
TV SHOWS

PLURAL NOUN _____

EXCLAMATION _____

PLURAL NOUN _____

PART OF THE BODY (PLURAL) _____

A PLACE _____

LAST NAME _____

PLURAL NOUN _____

A PLACE _____

LAST NAME _____

PLURAL NOUN _____

NOUN _____

PERSON IN ROOM _____

NOUN _____

VERB ENDING IN "S" _____

A PLACE _____

NOUN _____

PLURAL NOUN _____

NOUN _____

MAD LIBS
MIKE TEAVEE'S TV SHOWS

Here are a few of Mike Teavee's favorite television _____:
                                                    PLURAL NOUN

- _____ is a Western-style show about a family of
  EXCLAMATION

  wealthy _____ who wear cowboy hats on their
          PLURAL NOUN

  _____ and live on a ranch in (the) _____.
  PART OF THE BODY (PLURAL)   A PLACE

- _____'s Island follows the lives of seven shipwrecked
  LAST NAME

  _____ trying to survive on an island in the middle of
  PLURAL NOUN

  (the) _____.
        A PLACE

- The _____ Family is a television show about a kooky
      LAST NAME

  family with supernatural _____ who live in a haunted
                           PLURAL NOUN

  _____.
  NOUN

- Leave It to _____ follows a young boy nicknamed "The
              PERSON IN ROOM

  _____" as he _____ around his suburban
  NOUN   VERB ENDING IN "S"

  town.

- The _____ Hillbillies is about a very poor family who
      A PLACE

  stumble upon a/an _____ well, sell it for a million
                    NOUN

  _____, and move into a gigantic _____.
  PLURAL NOUN   NOUN

From CHARLIE AND THE CHOCOLATE FACTORY MAD LIBS® • Copyright © 2018 by
The Roald Dahl Story Company Limited. Published by Mad Libs, an imprint of Penguin Random House LLC.

MAD LIBS® is fun to play with friends, but you can also play it by yourself! To begin with, DO NOT look at the story on the page below. Fill in the blanks on this page with the words called for. Then, using the words you have selected, fill in the blank spaces in the story.

Now you've created your own hilarious MAD LIBS® game!

POOR MIKE TEAVEE

NOUN _____

PLURAL NOUN _____

ADJECTIVE _____

PLURAL NOUN _____

PLURAL NOUN _____

PART OF THE BODY (PLURAL) _____

NOUN _____

NOUN _____

EXCLAMATION _____

NOUN _____

NOUN _____

NOUN _____

NOUN _____

NOUN _____

PART OF THE BODY _____

MAD LIBS

POOR MIKE TEAVEE

When Mike Teavee won the fourth Golden _____ , his house
                                         NOUN
was filled with happy _____ . But Mike Teavee was annoyed
                        PLURAL NOUN
by the whole _____ business. "Can't you _____
                 ADJECTIVE   PLURAL NOUN
see I'm watching television?" he said angrily. You see, Mike Teavee was
head-over- _____ in love with television. He would watch
              PLURAL NOUN
it all day long with his _____ glued to the screen.
                          PART OF THE BODY (PLURAL)
So you can imagine Mike's excitement when he saw Willy Wonka
send a chocolate _____ through a television screen. "Could
                      NOUN
you send a real live person by television?" asked Mike. "That could be
very dangerous," Willy Wonka exclaimed. But Mike didn't care. He
pulled the switch on the _____ and— _____ !—
                              NOUN   EXCLAMATION
Mike was zapped by a/an _____ and shrank to the size of a
                             NOUN
tiny _____ ! "Oh, Mr. Wonka! How can we make him grow?"
        NOUN
his _____ wailed. "Well," said Mr. Wonka, stroking his
       NOUN
_____ thoughtfully, "we'll put him in a special machine I
     NOUN
have for testing the stretchiness of _____ gum and we'll stretch
                                       NOUN
his _____ back to size!"
    PART OF THE BODY

From CHARLIE AND THE CHOCOLATE FACTORY MAD LIBS® • Copyright © 2018 by
The Roald Dahl Story Company Limited. Published by Mad Libs, an imprint of Penguin Random House LLC.

MAD LIBS® is fun to play with friends, but you can also play it by yourself! To begin with, DO NOT look at the story on the page below. Fill in the blanks on this page with the words called for. Then, using the words you have selected, fill in the blank spaces in the story.

Now you've created your own hilarious MAD LIBS® game!

UP, UP, AND AWAY

NOUN _____

ADJECTIVE _____

NOUN _____

A PLACE _____

ADJECTIVE _____

NOUN _____

NOUN _____

A PLACE _____

PLURAL NOUN _____

ADJECTIVE _____

ADVERB _____

PART OF THE BODY (PLURAL) _____

MAD LIBS

UP, UP, AND AWAY

I, Charlie Bucket, was the last _____ standing at Willy
                                    NOUN
Wonka's Chocolate Factory. I could hardly believe my _____
                                                           ADJECTIVE
luck! Mr. Wonka whisked me and Grandpa Joe into the Great Glass

_____, where we went up, up, and away, crashing straight
   NOUN
through the ceiling of (the) _____ and into the sky! Down
                                  A PLACE
below, I could see all the other children and their _____
                                                           ADJECTIVE
families leaving the factory. That's when Mr. Wonka told me that he

was giving his beloved _____ to me! Little old Charlie
                            NOUN
_____! I must be the luckiest boy in (the) _____.
   NOUN   A PLACE
Then, the elevator crashed into my house, which splintered into teeny,

tiny _____. But much to my _____ surprise,
        PLURAL NOUN   ADJECTIVE
Mr. Wonka took my mum and dad and the rest of my grandparents

back to the factory. We were all going to live there, _____ ever
                                                            ADVERB
after! And we could eat all the chocolate our _____
                                                 PART OF THE BODY (PLURAL)
desired!

Download Mad Libs today!

Join the millions of Mad Libs fans creating wacky and wonderful stories on our apps!